REAL VICTORIANS

digital time traveller

Mike Corbishley

Illustrated by Dai Owen

ENGLISH HERITAGE

TAG Learning Ltd,
25 Pelham Road, Gravesend, Kent DA11 OHU

First published by TAG Publishing 2001
in association with English Heritage
10 9 8 7 6 5 4 3 2 1

Copyright © TAG Learning Ltd 2003
   Programming elements © TAG Learning 2003
   Illustrations © English Heritage 2003

A CIP catalogue record for this book
is available from the British Library

ISBN 1 902 804 11 2

Reprographics by Scanhouse UK Ltd
Printed in China by W K T

QuickTime   MADE WITH macromedia®

The Real Victorians team:

Text	**Mike Corbishley, English Heritage**
Cartoon illustrations	Dai Owen
Book design	Alan McPherson
Publishing Director	Kate Scarborough
CD concept work:	Mick Cooper
CD design & programming	Ultraviolet Design Ltd
VR photography	Martin Meyrick
Narrators	Jilly Bond & John Cording
Narration sound recording	Marall-Smith Studios, Keith Spillett
Music:	
Project co-ordinators	Helen Rudeforth & Ted Bunting
Technical support	Bernie Moore
Sound recording	Victoria Wright, Jon Bowen, Andrew Fisher, Helen Rudeforth & Ted Bunting
Performers	Laura & Jasper Bone, Hill Head School
	John Benbow, Jennie Coleman, Katherine Dennis, Robert Faulkner, Peter Flower, Jonathan Keane, Mark Rowley, Christopher Till, Paul Turner & Victoria Wright
Piano	Peter Flower
Harmonium	Christopher Till

Photography:
All English Heritage Photo Library or English Heritage Photo
Library/Skyscan Balloon Photography or English Heritage National
Monuments Record except for: Mary Evans Picture Library 8tl, 9tl & tr,
19tr, 34m & mr, 40 tr; Victoria & Albert Museum Picture Library 9tm, 14tr;
Royal Holloway & Bedford New College/The Bridgeman Art Library 9b;
Manchester City Art Galleries (details) 13tl & 29bl; Swindon Museum & Art
Gallery 20tr; National Railway Museum 21b; Lady Lever Art Gallery, Port
Sunlight/The Bridgeman Art Gallery 22; Wolverhampton Art Gallery/The
Bridgeman Art Library 28tr; The Royal Collection 38tl; Mike Corbishley 41
ml, br, 42 all; Norman Jacobs 41mr.

With thanks to Jennifer Ling and Richard Jones for allowing
their objects to be photographed for inclusion on page 43; to staff
and students in the Faculty of Education at the University of
Central England in Birmingham for performing and recording the
music; Steam – Museum of the Great Western Railway for access
to 34 Faringdon Road, Swindon.

Contents

Watch out for the CD buttons to get the most out of the tours, activities and references on the CD-ROM.

About Real Victorians

Real Victorians is part of the Digital Time Traveller series of interactive, history resources. The book, CD and web site have been designed to work together and provide everything you need to get started. The CD-ROM contains lots of useful things to help you to explore.

Top tours

There are four fantastic houses to visit on the CD-ROM: Osborne House, Brodsworth Hall, 34 Faringdon Road and Down House.

References

Examine the evidence for yourself! The CD-ROM includes additional information and resources, such as music, to help explain life in Victorian times.

Ace activities

There are five activities on the CD-ROM, including making your own Victorian e-cards. Of course, there are loads more things to make and do in this book – for example, why not play a game of ludo with a friend? (See page 27.) Time to get busy!

Crazy clip art

On the CD, you'll find lots of free clip art. How about making your own Victorian scrap book? With a little imagination, there's no limit to how you can use the pictures. (See page 42.)

Wicked websites

If you have access to the internet, there is a selection of brilliant websites to visit with facts about Victorians and their lives – all at the click of a button!

 Windows users

If you have a Windows PC you will need:
- a multimedia PC
- Windows '95 or higher
- CD-ROM drive
- super VGA monitor or better
- sound card with speakers or headphones
- 8MB available memory (RAM) (16MB recommended)

A printer, modem and Internet account will be useful for some of the on-screen activities.

Note: this is not a networkable product

 Apple Macintosh users

If you have a Macintosh you will need:
- 040 processor or better
- System 7.1 or above
- 640 x 480 monitor set to 256 or more colours
- CD-ROM drive
- speakers (usually built-in) or headphones
- 16MB available memory (RAM)

A printer, modem and Internet account will be useful for some of the on-screen activities.

Note: this is not a networkable product

Getting started

- Put the CD into your CD-drive (label-side up)
- Double click on My Computer, and then on your CD icon which will be called 'Victorians'
- Double click on the icon 'setup.exe'
- Follow the on-screen instructions

Starting Real Victorians
- Click on 'Start' in the task bar
- In Programs go to 'Victorians'
- Double-click on 'Real Victorians Start'
If your computer does not have Quicktime™ installed, click on QuickTimeInstaller.exe.

 You do not need to install Real Victorians. It runs directly from the CD-drive.
- Put the Real Victorians CD into your CD-drive (with the label pointing up)
- Open the CD from the desktop
- Double-click on the 'Real Victorians' icon
If you would like to install Real Victorians, copy the files to your hard drive and play from there.

Using the CD-ROM

Finding your way around the CD-ROM is easy. Just click on the theatre characters and you will discover the main sections.

Guided tours

Click on each adult to visit their home. The butler takes you to Brodsworth Hall; Queen Victoria will show you around Osborne House; Emma Darwin invites you in to Down House and the railwayman takes you into his home in Swindon.

Moving around the Victorian sites is easy. Just click on the square buttons down the sides to go to all the rooms available to view. If you want to go back to the

beginning click on the home button; if you want to go to Activities click on the spinning top button and for References, click on the pile of books button.

Once in a room, you can look all the way around by clicking down with your mouse and moving it to the left or right, up or down. There are hotspots in each room, so watch for the cursor to change into a hand and click down to find out more about that object. Keep hunting for extra info!

Activities

Click the boy to select one of the on-screen activities, such as a quiz or jigsaw. The Activities section also provides a library of useful clip art that you can use in your own work. This is in JPEG format and can be imported into other applications.

References

Click on the girl for additional information, facts and pictures on Victorian topics, such as exploration, schools, transport, food and the Great Exhibition.

On the Website

For further information, there are also a number of useful Internet links, accessed directly from the Real Victorian web page (see page 44.) Always remember to tell an adult when you are going on-line. Of course, the best way to find out about Real Victorians is to sit back and explore...

Who were the Victorians?

We call the period of British history in the 19th century 'Victorian' because from 1837 to 1901 Britain was ruled by Queen Victoria.

During Victoria's reign thousands of people moved out of the country into the towns and cities. This busy London street in the late 19th century shows horse-drawn omnibuses carrying commuters to their offices and shops.

Queen Victoria not only ruled Britain but an enormous empire of countries right across the world (see page 32). During Victoria's reign many significant changes took place in Britain and elsewhere. By the end of her reign, for example, people travelled in steam ships across the world's oceans, not sailing ships. In the 19th century steam trains replaced horse-drawn stage coaches, electricity replaced gas lighting and the motor car was invented.

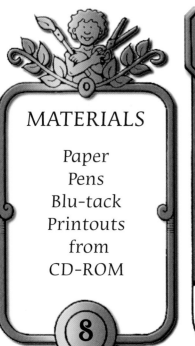

MAKE YOUR OWN WALL TIMELINE

MATERIALS

Paper
Pens
Blu-tack
Printouts
from
CD-ROM

Print off the timeline information and the pictures from clipart.

Make a wall timeline out of paper, draw on main dates.

Stick up pictures. Stand back and admire.

Famous Victorians

Many famous men and women in British history lived and worked in Victoria's reign.

The founder of professional nursing, Florence Nightingale, fought to provide better medical care for soldiers in the Crimean War. After the war she set up a school for nurses.

The most popular Victorian novels were written by Charles Dickens (see page 40). His books were first published as serials in magazines.

The engineer, Isambard Kingdom Brunel designed railways (see page 20), bridges and steamships, including the famous SS Great Western, the first transatlantic liner.

BELOW: Paddington Station, London, painted by William Powell Frith in 1862. Cheap train fares meant that the Victorians could travel easily and quickly all over the country.

RIGHT: The scientist Charles Darwin published his important work on evolution (see page 31).

While Victoria reigned........

Many of the buildings and the new inventions which were used in Victoria's reign are still part of our everyday lives...

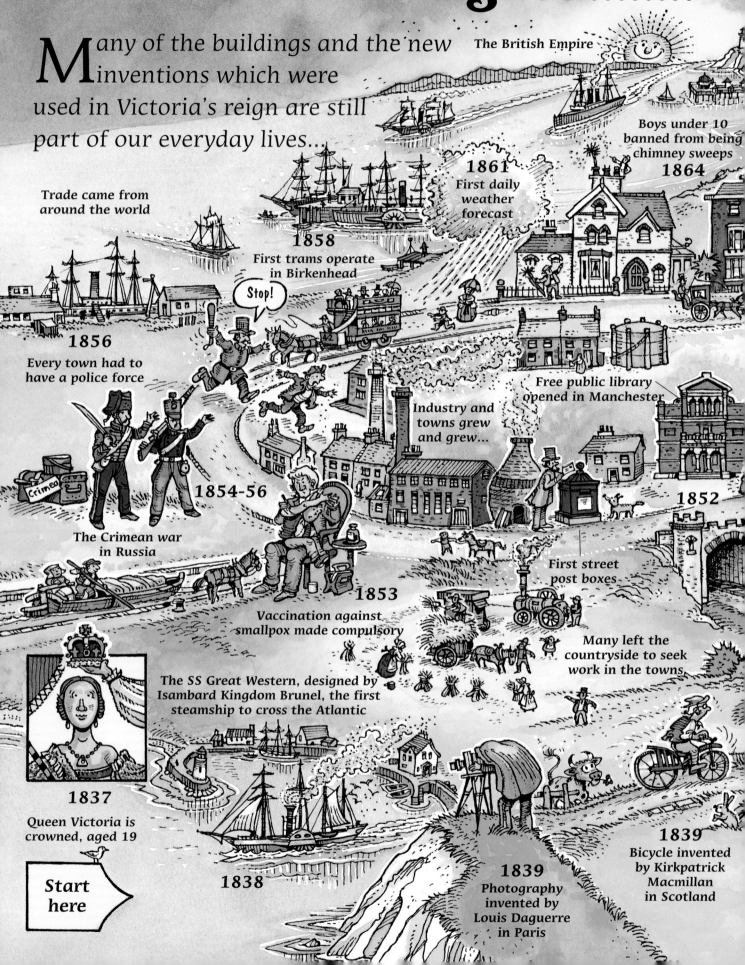

The British Empire

Boys under 10 banned from being chimney sweeps
1864

1861
First daily weather forecast

Trade came from around the world

1858
First trams operate in Birkenhead

Stop!

1856
Every town had to have a police force

Free public library opened in Manchester

Industry and towns grew and grew...

1854-56
The Crimean war in Russia

Crimea

1852

First street post boxes

1853
Vaccination against smallpox made compulsory

Many left the countryside to seek work in the towns

The SS Great Western, designed by Isambard Kingdom Brunel, the first steamship to cross the Atlantic

1837
Queen Victoria is crowned, aged 19

Start here

1838

1839
Photography invented by Louis Daguerre in Paris

1839
Bicycle invented by Kirkpatrick Macmillan in Scotland

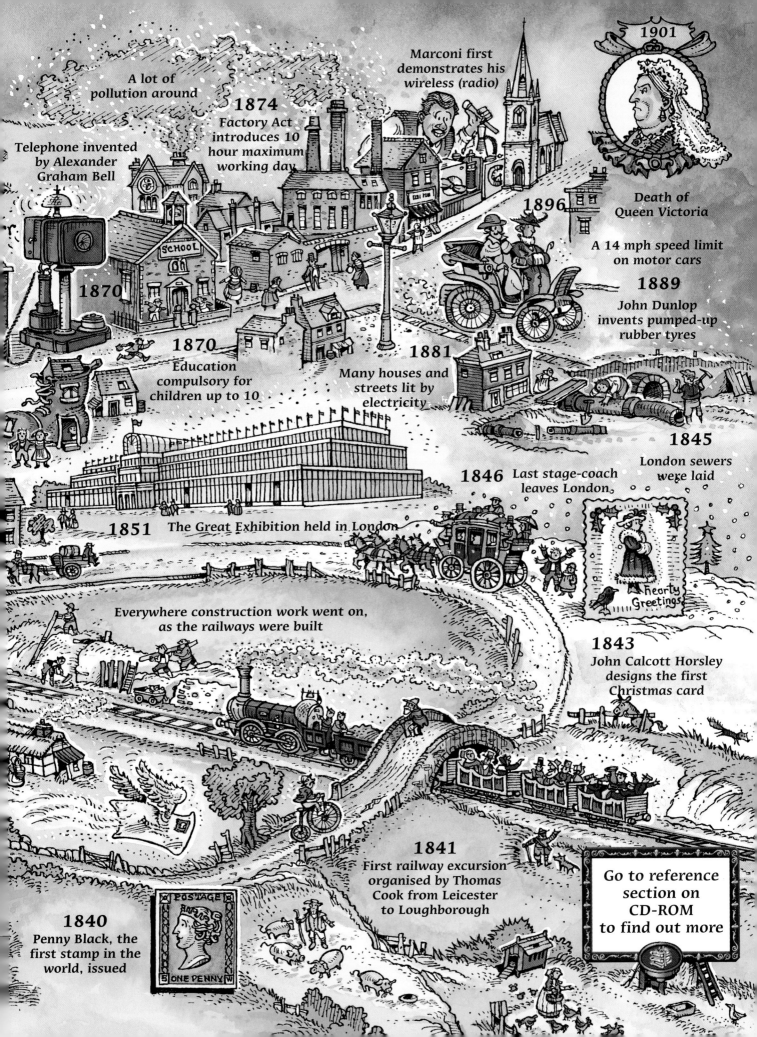

Victorian society

Although life was comfortable for rich Victorians, the poor worked long hours just to earn enough money to provide themselves with food, shelter and clothes.

Gathering in the hay on a Victorian farm.

At the start of the 19th century most people lived in the countryside as they were needed to work the land. But as farms used more machinery fewer men were needed and country families had to look for employment elsewhere. Their houses were usually tied to the man's job so they had to look for a house as well.

To make matters worse, the population of Britain doubled in Victoria's reign and was about 40 million by the time she died. Most people had to live in towns in order to find work in the factories. They lived in rows of small houses built close to the place of work.

At work

Factories and coal-mines were dangerous and unhealthy places to work in. Gradually Acts of Parliament, which helped working people, and child workers in particular, were passed in the 19th century. For example, by 1887 boys under 13 could not work in mines.

MATERIALS

Printouts
from
CD-ROM
Card & glue
Scissors
Black paint
Thread

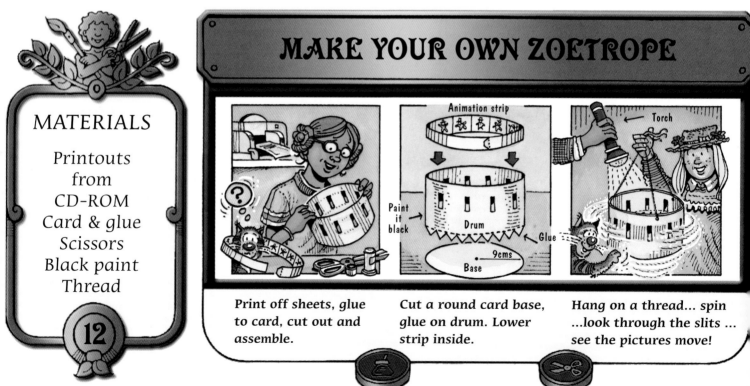

MAKE YOUR OWN ZOETROPE

Animation strip

Paint it black

Drum

Glue

9cms

Base

Torch

Print off sheets, glue to card, cut out and assemble.

Cut a round card base, glue on drum. Lower strip inside.

Hang on a thread... spin ...look through the slits ... see the pictures move!

An Oxfordshire mill-worker making blankets in 1898.

'Work' by Ford Madox Brown shows the three classes in Victorian society. The upper classes are at the top, while middle class ladies watch the workers below.

Class

One of the biggest changes which took place in Victorian times was that people saw themselves as belonging to a particular 'class' of society. The 'upper class' still owned most of the land and held all the important positions in the government. A 'middle class' had arisen. They earned their money in trade or in office jobs. The 'working class' provided the manual labour needed in factories and on the land.

Religion

At least half of the people in Victorian Britain went to church on Sundays. New churches had to be built for the huge populations in towns and cities. Some Christian groups did not want to worship in Church of England or Roman Catholic churches and built their own chapels or meeting houses.

REPENT!

Health and medicine

In early Victorian times huge numbers of people died from diseases which can be cured easily today.

New discoveries

There was no National Health Service in the 19th century and many people, especially the poor, had to buy cheap remedies from untrained doctors or 'quacks'. Two major discoveries cut down the risk to patients who had operations. In 1847 James Simpson used chloroform as an anaesthetic to relieve pain. In 1867 Joseph Lister developed an antiseptic spray which killed bacteria. Before his discovery more than half of the

Untrained doctors sold medicines on the street, like this one here photographed in 1877.

patients who had undergone surgery died from shock or from infections.

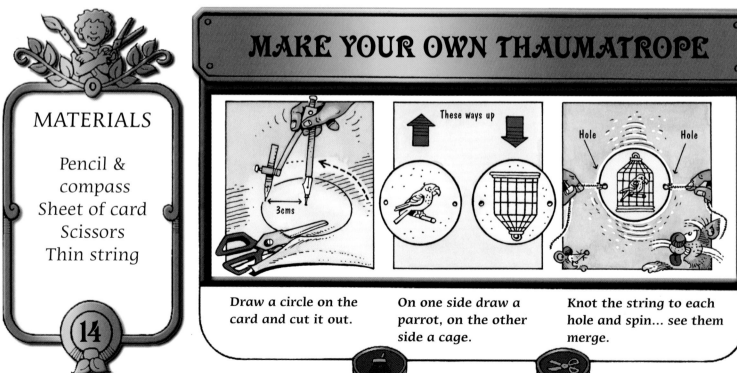

MATERIALS

Pencil & compass
Sheet of card
Scissors
Thin string

MAKE YOUR OWN THAUMATROPE

These ways up

Hole   Hole

Draw a circle on the card and cut it out.

On one side draw a parrot, on the other side a cage.

Knot the string to each hole and spin... see them merge.

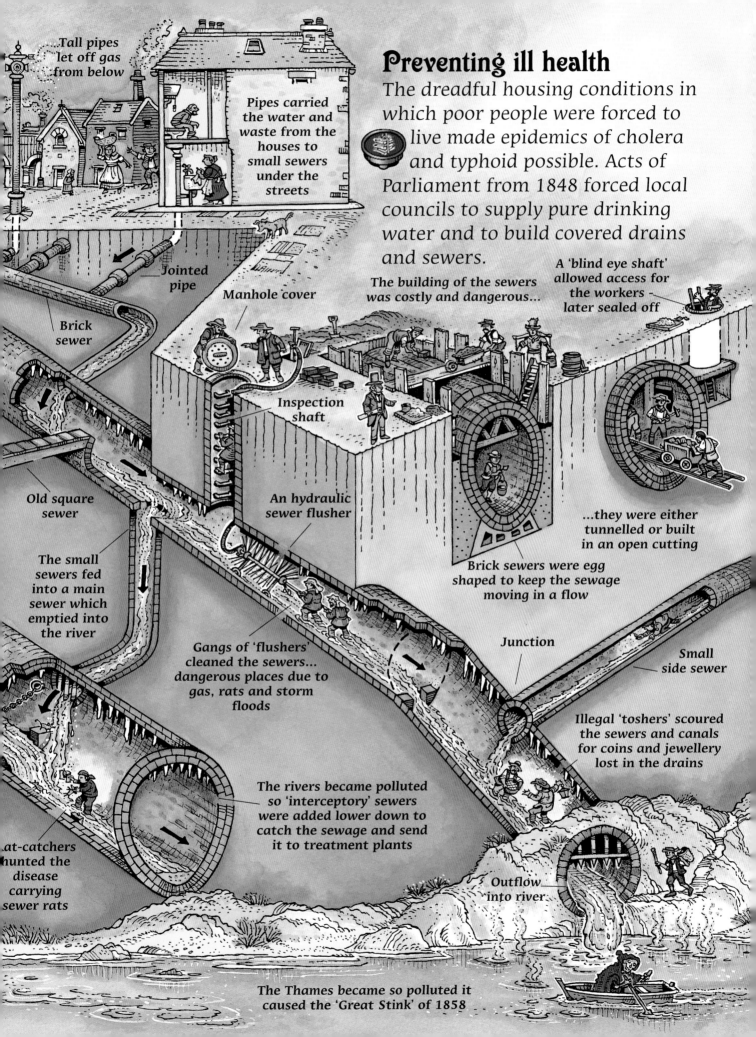

Tall pipes let off gas from below

Pipes carried the water and waste from the houses to small sewers under the streets

Preventing ill health

The dreadful housing conditions in which poor people were forced to live made epidemics of cholera and typhoid possible. Acts of Parliament from 1848 forced local councils to supply pure drinking water and to build covered drains and sewers.

The building of the sewers was costly and dangerous...

A 'blind eye shaft' allowed access for the workers - later sealed off

Jointed pipe

Manhole cover

Brick sewer

Inspection shaft

Old square sewer

An hydraulic sewer flusher

...they were either tunnelled or built in an open cutting

Brick sewers were egg shaped to keep the sewage moving in a flow

The small sewers fed into a main sewer which emptied into the river

Gangs of 'flushers' cleaned the sewers... dangerous places due to gas, rats and storm floods

Junction

Small side sewer

Illegal 'toshers' scoured the sewers and canals for coins and jewellery lost in the drains

The rivers became polluted so 'interceptory' sewers were added lower down to catch the sewage and send it to treatment plants

...at-catchers hunted the disease carrying sewer rats

Outflow into river

The Thames became so polluted it caused the 'Great Stink' of 1858

The Midland Grand Hotel was built in 1874 for passengers who used St Pancras railway station in London.

'Board' schools were built all over the country after 1870. Many, like this one in Wandsworth, London, are still in use.

Victorian streets were lit by gas lamps. Some, like these, also took gas off from sewers under the street.

City living

Many of the changes in Victorian cities can still be seen today. Many of our public buildings, such as museums, libraries, hospitals and town halls were built in the second half of the 19th century.

Victorian streets were busy places filled with traders selling anything from milk to flowers or hot pies or a shoeshine. In the centre of cities there were not only houses and flats but factories

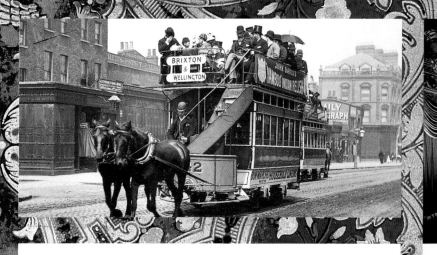

Inside a richly decorated Victorian theatre - the Hackney Empire, London. The auditorium held 2,500 people.

and workshops. There were also shopping streets and impressive banks and new office buildings.

Local politicians, who usually owned the area's industries, often wanted to build something for poorer people. To be sure that their generosity was appreciated, these buildings nearly always had their name on it. Sir Henry Tate, who made his wealth from sugar, built free public libraries. George Peabody built blocks of 'model dwellings' for working-class families. In almost every town and city public parks, art galleries and theatres were being built in Victorian times.

This impressive public library was built in 1893 for the people who lived in one part of the city of Birmingham.

The Royal Waterloo Hospital for Women and Children, in Lambeth, London, began as a dispensary for children in 1822.

Getting around

It was during Victoria's reign that a transport revolution took place. More people than ever before were able to travel by the new forms of transport.

Personal transport

The invention of the bicycle brought a cheap form of transport to thousands. James Starley invented the penny-farthing (named after the largest and smallest coins then in use) in 1870. But it was his nephew John Starley who first manufactured the modern form of bicycle - the Rover 'safety bicycle' - in 1885. In the late 19th century the motor car gave a few rich people the opportunity to travel to more places across the country.

Cyclists in Hyde Park, London, in the 1890s.

Public transport

While horses were still used right through the Victorian period, other ways of travelling were invented or developed. At first there were horse-drawn trams (on rails) or horse omnibuses (on roads). By 1855 omnibuses were carrying 20,000 people a day in London.

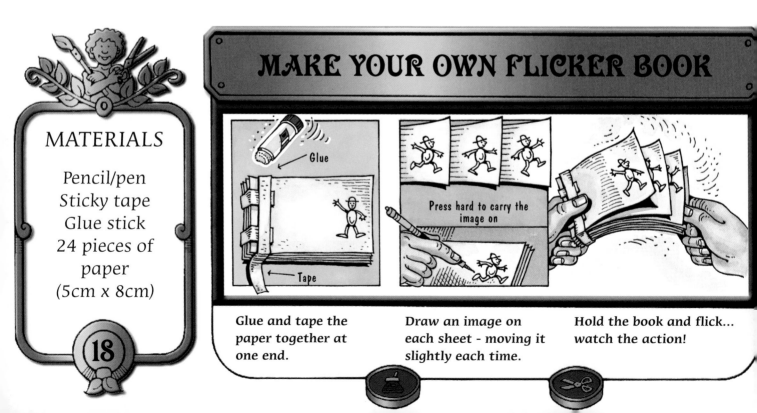

MAKE YOUR OWN FLICKER BOOK

MATERIALS

Pencil/pen
Sticky tape
Glue stick
24 pieces of paper
(5cm x 8cm)

Glue

Tape

Press hard to carry the image on

Glue and tape the paper together at one end.

Draw an image on each sheet - moving it slightly each time.

Hold the book and flick... watch the action!

Railways

Even before Victoria came to the throne, there had been a railway system in England. The world's first public railway was opened between Darlington and Stockton in 1825. The railways were used to transport food, goods and materials as well as passengers from town to town.

In Britain between 1844 and 1848 there was an enormous expansion of the railways. So many new lines were constructed that people called it 'railway mania'. By 1852 all the main British railway routes had been built.

The invention of electricity made it possible for the first underground railway in the world to be built in London in 1862.

The men who dug the cuttings and the bridges and tunnels were called navigators or navvies for short.

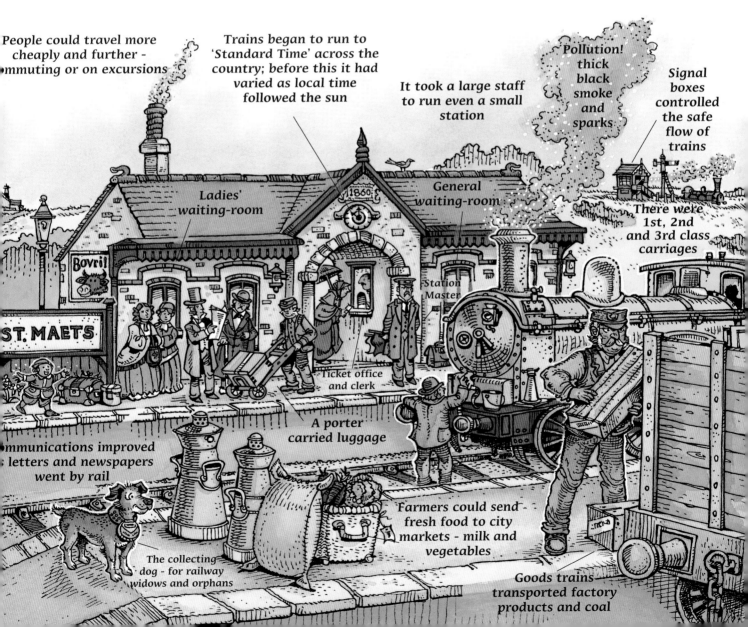

People could travel more cheaply and further - commuting or on excursions

Trains began to run to 'Standard Time' across the country; before this it had varied as local time followed the sun

It took a large staff to run even a small station

Pollution! thick black smoke and sparks

Signal boxes controlled the safe flow of trains

Ladies' waiting-room

1860

General waiting-room

There were 1st, 2nd and 3rd class carriages

Bovril

Station Master

ST. MAETS

Ticket office and clerk

A porter carried luggage

Communications improved - letters and newspapers went by rail

The collecting dog - for railway widows and orphans

Farmers could send fresh food to city markets - milk and vegetables

Goods trains transported factory products and coal

From the middle of the 19th century a whole new town at Swindon in Wiltshire was built just for the workers and staff of the Great Western Railway's engineering works and station.

In 1833 a new company, the Great Western Railway, was set up to build a railway connection between Bristol and London. Isambard Kingdom Brunel was appointed as the engineer. The company needed a large engineering works to build and maintain its engines and carriages. The company bought open farmland and, because there were no skilled workers anywhere in the area, provided houses for the workers they brought to Swindon. When the first houses were built

A painting of the proposed new railway works and village at Swindon by Edward Snell in 1849.

there were 663 employees. When Queen Victoria and Prince Albert stopped at Swindon station on their way from the Isle of Wight (see page 38) to Scotland in 1852, there were

MAKE YOUR OWN WALL MOTTO

MATERIALS

Printouts from
CD-ROM
Card
Colour pencils
Scissors
Glue

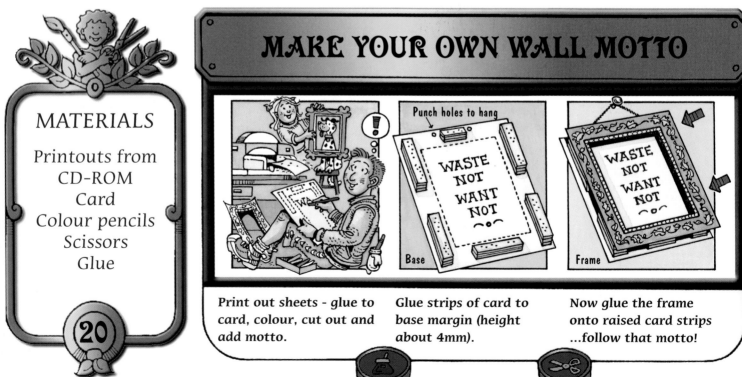

Print out sheets - glue to card, colour, cut out and add motto.

Glue strips of card to base margin (height about 4mm).

Now glue the frame onto raised card strips ...follow that motto!

34 Faringdon Road, Swindon. RIGHT: *Parlour.*

nearly 2,000 employees.

The new railway village gradually grew into a town to provide houses for the workers. The  furnished house at 34 Faringdon Road was one of a block built in 1846-7. A skilled railway worker or foreman and his family, and probably a lodger as well, lived in this small house.

Town facilities

But the town needed more than just houses. The company built shops, a public house, a church and a school. The town grew, and by 1893 there were 10,000 employees. There were also chapels, several more schools, a hospital, a Mechanics' Institution, a town hall, a swimming-pool and a public park.

The Mechanics Institution was built in 1854-5 as a place for railway workers to go to relax and to be educated. The building had a reading-room, dining and coffee rooms, baths (because houses and lodgings had no bathrooms) and a regular programme of lectures and concerts.

Clothes and fashion

In Victorian times it was easy to tell which class a person belonged to from the sort of clothes she or he wore.

As the Victorian period lasted over 60 years fashions changed, especially for the rich. In the 1850s women were still wearing crinoline dresses made from petticoats and skirt over steel or whalebone hoops. By the end of Victoria's reign styles were simpler and less formal. Women cyclists even wore knickerbocker dresses or bloomers, invented by an American, Mrs Amelia Jenks Bloomer.

Boys and girls both wore dresses until they were about five years old. Working people wore simpler clothes and ones suitable for the job

'Boulter's Lock, Sunday afternoon' painted in 1895 by Edward John Gregory. Going on a trip was a chance to show off 'Sunday best' clothes.

they did - housemaids wore starched aprons but gardeners, for example, wore strong corduroy trousers and waistcoats. People from all classes tried to keep a set of clothes for 'Sunday best'.

MAKE YOUR OWN BATHING BELLE

MATERIALS

Printouts from the CD-ROM
Glue
Card
6 paper studs
Thread

...and open

Push stud through

back view

Thread

Print off the drawing from CD-ROM, colour in and glue to card.

Cut out ...pierce holes at the 12 dots and attach together with studs.

Connect the parts with thread (as above) and see her jig!

... Stepping out

Clothing for men and women, and for the rich and the poor, was very different

1840

1890

UPPER CLASS COUPLES

Men wore darker clothes

Women wore bows and ribbons

Fashion changed over the years

MIDDLE CLASS COUPLE

Less showy clothes

LADY CYCLIST

Clothes had to adapt

SHOP KEEPER

Aprons were worn for work

A child was dressed like a small adult

ASSISTANT UNDER-BUTLER

Some jobs had uniforms suited to their work

Hats were popular

MAID-SERVANT

BEACH HUT ATTENDANT

The clothing trade used a variety of skills

Brodsworth Hall

The owner of the estate at Brodsworth, Charles Thellusson, decided to knock down the 18th-century house there in 1859 and to build a grand but more comfortable and up-to-date home for his family with enough room for his servants.

By today's standards it is a huge house for a family with six children but there were also at least fifteen servants who cleaned, cooked, tended the garden and cared for the family and their guests. The garden was laid out in favourite Victorian styles.

ABOVE: **Charles Thellusson.**

A Thellusson family photo album from around 1870.

The house was in the centre of a large area of formal gardens, woodlands, and parkland.

Feeding the family

In a wing at the back of the house were the rooms where the house servants prepared the meals for family and guests. There is a larder for cold storage, a huge kitchen, the butler's pantry (where the cutlery, glasses and silver plate were stored and cleaned), a sitting room for the housekeeper and a servant's hall (where all the servants took their meals).

MAKE YOUR OWN SUGAR MICE

MATERIALS

White of 1 egg
3 cups of icing sugar
Peppermint flavouring
Food colouring
String

Beat the colouring, flavouring and egg together in a bowl.

Sprinkle icing sugar and mix until stiff... shape into mice.

Make holes for eyes... dip string in water and press in for tail.

A Victorian painting of Brodsworth Hall.

The formal gardens at Brodsworth with the house in the background.

Large 'Eagle' cast-iron cooking range

Baking oven

Warming shelf

Hatch for taking food to the dining room

Clock - timing was important

Gas lighting

Dressers held copper and cast-iron pots and pans

Mincer

Moveable meat screen

Hot plate

Cook was in charge

Coal scuttle

Firebox

Scales for weighing

Scullery maid

Kitchen maid

Jelly moulds

Ovens for roasting

Almo

Recipe book

FLOUR

RAISI

Reflecting oven - the meat revolved

Pastimes and games

The first public holidays were introduced for working people in 1871 - Bank Holidays - and thousands went for a day at the seaside by railway.

But going to the seaside was not the only entertainment on offer. Victorian families could go to the circus or a fair, watch cricket and football matches, be entertained by song and dance shows at the theatre or music hall or visit the new museums and art galleries.

Weymouth beach in late Victorian times.

At home

 Favourite pastimes for families were singing around a piano, reading aloud from novels and stories or playing card games and board games such as Ludo.

A selection of games played by the children at Brodsworth Hall. The two games on the left - making houses from building blocks - were very popular with Victorian children.

MAKE YOUR OWN THEATRE

MATERIALS

Print out sheets
from CD-ROM
Glue
Card
Colour pencils
Scissors
Straws

Print out the sheets, glue to card and colour.

Cut out the theatre - fold back stage, glue in supports.

Cut out actors - fasten to straws ...curtain up!

Ludo

A rich American, George Peabody, gave £500,000 in 1864 to put up 'Peabody Dwellings' for poor families in London.

Part of an elaborately painted wall at Brodsworth Hall. The painting was stencilled and given a marble effect.

Victorian houses were built in the suburbs for middle-class families in all sorts of sizes and styles.

Houses & homes

One of the biggest differences between Victorian houses and ours today is in the enormous amount of elaborate decoration which covered the insides and outsides of most buildings.

In most Victorian houses, both large and small, the sitting room was very important. Down House (page 30) and the railway worker's house in Swindon (page 20) have a room set aside for relaxing after work,

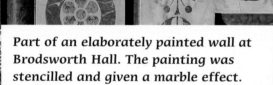

conversation or family pastimes. Each room in a Victorian house would be decorated and furnished in a particular way.

The Victorians liked ornaments, both inside and outside their houses. The rich could afford to buy beautiful pottery or glass objects, or even statues and paintings. The poor had to make do with calendars from shops or factories, their own embroidered pictures, quotations and small pottery figures.  On the outside of houses and other buildings were all sorts of decorative features – columns, decorated bricks or tiles, figures or faces and elaborate name and date plaques.

Victorian houses often had brightly coloured tiled floors, especially in the entrance hall and outside the front door.

Part of a carpet from the drawing room at Brodsworth Hall. This was called 'Extra Fine Real Axminster' carpet.

Estates of houses were built in Victorian times. 2,000 of these two-storey houses were built for skilled workers.

Down House

I n 1842 the scientist Charles Darwin decided he needed a family house away from London to carry out his experiments and to write in peace and quiet. He chose Down House in a small country village in Kent, only 16 miles from London.

The house itself was not big enough for Darwin's family and servants and he set about extending it, including a schoolroom for the children, a larger kitchen, a butlers' hall and of course a study.

A painting of Down House in 1880.

The family man

But Charles Darwin did not just lock himself away with his scientific work. He did not mind his children (Charles and Emma had ten children) playing noisily in the house or even coming into his study to fetch things.

Scientific work

Charles Darwin had already carried out scientific work long before he came to Down House. He was the

MAKE YOUR OWN BOOK OF SCRAPS

MATERIALS

6 A4 sheets of paper
Needle & thread
Print scraps off CD-ROM
Glue

Fold the paper and punch 3 holes in the central ridge.

Stitch them together to form a book (as above).

Now stick in the scraps and start your album.

scientist on board HMS Beagle on its voyage of discovery to Tierra del Fuego (see next page) from 1831 to 1836. He collected many specimens and made notes. He had begun to work out theories about how species of animals had developed in different environments.

Beetles collected by Charles Darwin.

Darwin was also very interested in earthworms. The whole family joined in his experiments on worms in flower pots on the piano by playing their musical instruments to find out if worms could hear! Darwin discovered that worms could not hear but did react to the vibrations of the piano.

Charles Darwin's family around 1870. Emma Darwin is sitting down with a dog at her feet.

Daily routine

Darwin had a regular daily routine. In the morning he would work in his study and listen to his wife, Emma reading out family letters. Before lunch he always went for a walk around the 'Sandwalk' in his garden to think about his work. From lunch until 7.30pm he read or wrote letters (he wrote about 7000 letters and postcards in his lifetime!), listened to Emma reading aloud, rested or worked in his study.

The 'Sandwalk', Darwin's 'thinking path'.

Charles Darwin corresponded with many other scientists, often by postcard as here.

Exploration and empire

In the 19th century Britain, as well as other countries, established their rule over many other parts of the world. The British Empire was always marked pink on maps at the time.

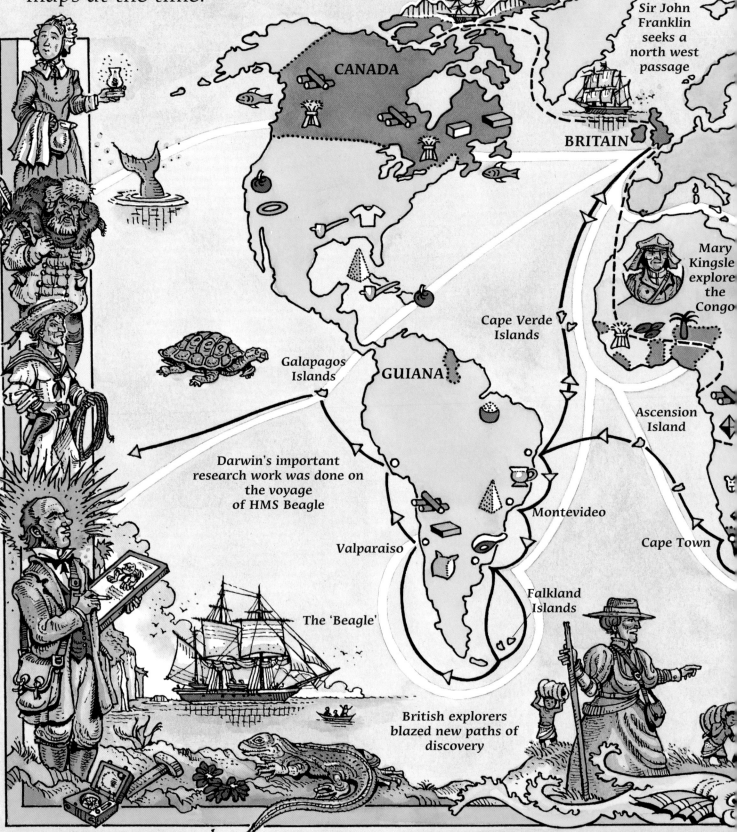

Sir John Franklin seeks a north west passage

CANADA

BRITAIN

Mary Kingsle explore the Congo

Cape Verde Islands

Galapagos Islands

GUIANA

Ascension Island

Montevideo

Cape Town

Darwin's important research work was done on the voyage of HMS Beagle

Valparaiso

Falkland Islands

The 'Beagle'

British explorers blazed new paths of discovery

All kinds of goods were imported from across the globe

Francis Younghusband crosses the Gobi desert

EGYPT

INDIA

Hong Kong

The main world trade routes were controlled by Britain's colonies

John Speke explores Lake Victoria

Dr Livingstone, a missionary, travels across Africa

SOUTH AFRICA

The Beagle's route

AUSTRALIA

Sydney

NEW ZEALAND

British rule was enforced by her army and navy

Go to reference section on CD-ROM to find out more

Inventions and discoveries

Victorians were fascinated by all the new inventions, especially by gadgets which they could use themselves - from telephones to carpet-sweepers.

Improvements in the house

Many of the things you can find in your kitchen today were invented in Victorian times. In the early 19th century food was cooked on a coal-fired iron 'range'. By the 1880s many types of gas cookers were available and ten years later some kitchens had electric cookers.

Gadgets of all sorts were also on sale, from mechanical apple peelers to knife cleaners and meat mincers, called 'food choppers'. Machines were also invented for housework. Carpet-sweepers first appeared in the 1870s along with water-powered washing-machines. By the end of Victoria's reign housemaids were even using hand-pumped vacuum cleaners!

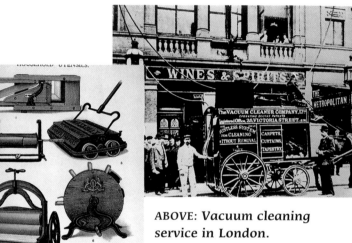

ABOVE: Vacuum cleaning service in London.
LEFT: 1 Bread cutter. 2 Coffee roaster. 3 Carpet sweeper. 4 Wringer and mangle. 5 Knife cleaner. 6 Spice box.

MAKE YOUR OWN TELEPHONE

MATERIALS

2 plastic cups or cartons
String
(5-10 metres)

Pierce a small hole in the base of each cup.

Push the string through each hole and tie a knot.

Keep string tight

Now pull the line tight ...and communicate!

The Great Exhibition

All the latest inventions and advances in technology were put on show on 1 May 1851 inside the world's largest cast-iron and glass building. The Great Exhibition was dreamed up by Prince Albert. The Crystal Palace, as the building was called, was designed by Joseph Paxton and had over 13,000 exhibits from Britain and around the world. Six million visitors came to Hyde Park in London to see the Great Exhibition which was open for 20 weeks.

After Prince Albert died in 1861 a memorial to him was built in Hyde Park.

The Great Exhibition covered 6 times the area of St. Pauls Cathedral and enclosed 3 of the Park's great elm trees

The parts were mass produced and easily assembled: there were 300,000 panes of glass

The displays were very varied ranging from a steam train to the Koh-i-nor diamond -

The visitors ate all kinds of food including 2 million buns!

There were worries that the countless vibration would shatter the glass

Queen Victoria visited it often - nearly every day

People travelled from all over Britain, often by cheap special excursions, to see it

There was a huge Exhibition Hall with a cast-iron fountain, statues and displays on different levels.

Going to school

Because of a new law passed in 1870 education had to be provided by local boards of governors for all children between five and 13 years old. This is a typical 'board' school......

Bell summoned children to school

High brick wall

The 'Kid-Catcher' hunted the truants

Her Majesty's Inspector tested them in the 3 Rs - Reading 'Riting 'Rithmetic

1872

Ink monitor

SCHOOL YARD

The bell was rung to summon children into class

Bad work meant shame and the Dunce's hat

The Standards (classes) marched into school in single file

Many games were played in the lunch break

Often children were in rags and bare feet

The Standards were often taught in one large room

ler children te carefully pen and ink copy books'

Young children learnt to write on sandtrays and slates

MORE HASTE LESS SPEED

Empire

Windows were high up to cut out the view

Stove for heating

$2 \times 2 = 4$
$3 \times 2 = 6$
$4 \times 2 = 8$

A monitor - about 9 years old teaches the others

Spell abcd efgh

Metal framed wooden desks

The register

The teacher watched all from his high chair

Blackboard and chalk

A young pil teacher

bles were learnt rote' - repeating r and over - very noisy

Bible

Bell

Punishment book and cane

An abacus - a calculator using beads

Playing skittles

Wooden dumb-bells

Go to reference section on CD-ROM to find out more

Drill - they did exercises in lines - a very regimental PE!

Osborne House

Queen Victoria never liked the royal palaces where she was expected to live. In 1845 she and Prince Albert bought an old house and estate on the Isle of Wight, off the south coast, and built themselves a place of their own by the seaside.

Victoria and Albert employed the London building contractor Thomas Cubitt to build them a new house and demolish the old one. The prince and Thomas Cubitt worked closely together to provide family rooms and areas for state receptions and banquets. A home farm supplied Osborne with daily produce. Finally Osborne House was as Victoria wanted 'a place of one's own, quiet and retired'. Victoria spent as much time

An aerial view of Osborne House with its formal gardens at the back of the house.

as she could on the Isle of Wight. She died in her own bedroom at Osborne on 22 January 1901.

MAKE YOUR OWN BEACH FLAGS

MATERIALS

Paper
Pens
Sticks
or straws
Glue

Bend here

Glue sides together

Draw flags (both sides) of any nation on paper and colour.

Glue each flag onto kebab stick or plastic straw.

Stick in sand-castle or in a flowerpot in your bedroom.

The royal children

Although Victoria had state business to attend to while at Osborne she spent as much time as she could with Albert and their children. She helped them with their lessons and on most evenings they all came in turn (the youngest first) to visit her. Albert engaged in all sorts of games with the children - from flying kites to making snowmen.

Nursery rooms

Just like other upper-class families, the children of Victoria and Albert lived in their own special suite of rooms. The children's rooms were on the floor just above their parents' private rooms. There was a nursery sitting room with small-size furniture. The nursery bedroom has a swing cradle for a baby, two children's cots and a bed for the children's nurse.

Sea bathing

Bathing in the sea became very popular in Victorian times. The first time Queen Victoria swam in the sea was at Osborne in 1847. She wrote 'I thought it delightful till I put my head under the water, when I thought I should be stifled'.

In the garden

Albert created a special area of the garden for the children. He encouraged them to find out about business by growing vegetables and selling them to the estate. They had their own little summer-house with small garden tools and wheelbarrows, painted with each child's initials.

Swiss Cottage, a miniature replica of a Swiss timber house which was given to the royal children on Victoria's birthday in 1854. INSET: Living room at Swiss Cottage.

Find Victorian documents

An enormous number of real Victorian documents survive today - you may even find some in your own house together with your old family photographs!

Victorian books

The Victorians published a huge number of books and magazines for every class in society, from 'The Servant's Magazine' to science fiction such as Jules Verne's 'Twenty Thousand Leagues under the Sea' and H G Wells' 'The First Men on the Moon'. The famous Victorian writer, Charles Dickens, originally published his books

('A Christmas Carol', 'Oliver Twist' and 'The Pickwick Papers', for example) as episodes in magazines and gave public readings of his latest novels.

Photography

Although the world's first photograph was taken by the Frenchman Niepce in 1826, it was during Victorian times photography became very popular. William Henry Fox Talbot invented a system of fixing images on paper to produce negatives in 1839. Now large numbers of prints could be made.

MATERIALS

Cardboard box
Greaseproof paper
Baking foil
Tape

MAKE YOUR OWN CAMERA

Replace 2 opposite sides of box... one with greaseproof paper.

...the other with foil with a pinhole in the centre.

Point the pinhole at a window and see the upside-down image.

Here are a variety of Victorian documents. But what is a document? As well as printed books documents can be paintings or photographs because they will give us evidence of what Victorian life was like.

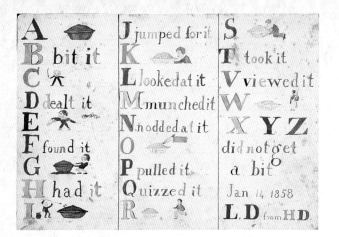

An alphabet scrapbook belonging to one of Charles Darwin's children.

Adverts appeared in all magazines and newspapers but also in the front and back pages of books.

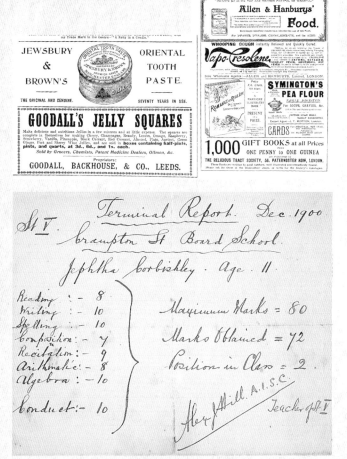

A school report for a boy attending a 'board school' in London in 1900.

A postcard sent in 1901. On holiday at the seaside resort of Clacton-on-Sea.

The latest fashions for ladies from the May 1863 issue of 'English Woman's Domestic Magazine'.

All the family are wearing their 'Sunday Best' at this Victorian wedding.

Be a Victorian archaeologist

You are certain to find some clues to Victorian life in the area you live in. Look out for them on the street and in the buildings around you.

Plaque on a house.

You will probably find a few Victorian buildings in your town. Look out especially for public buildings, such as libraries, museums, art galleries and town halls. But how do you know whether they were built in Victorian times? The first clue to look out for is a plaque on the wall with a date on it - if it is any time between Victoria becoming queen in 1837 and her death in 1901, the building is Victorian.

In the street

You will often find evidence for the Victorians in the street. Look out for letter-boxes with the letters VR, standing for Victoria Regina ('regina' is the Latin word for queen), like the one here. Notice street or public park names too - 'Victoria' is an obvious one. 'Jubilee' was a very popular street name and looks back to Victoria's Golden Jubilee celebrated in 1887 after 50 years of her reign.

JUBILEE STREET

MAKE YOUR OWN CHRISTMAS CARD

MATERIALS

Victorian cards
from
CD-ROM
Colour pencils
Sheet of card
Envelopes
Stamps

Print off real Victorian cards from CD-ROM.

Use as inspiration... Draw and colour your own designs.

Post them to your friends - Merry Christmas!

Mystery objects

Can you guess what these
Victorian objects were used for?
Check your answers on page 48.

1

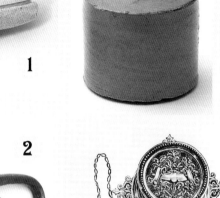

2

3

4

5

6

7

8

9

10

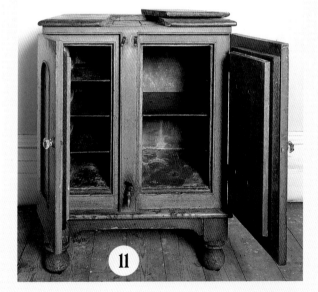

11

12

Real Victorians on the web

If you have an Internet connection you can find out lots more about Victorians on-line. This section contains a selection of useful links to important castle web sites.

You will need
- a modem connected to your PC
- a Web Browser
  (such as Netscape Navigator, or Internet Explorer)
- an Internet service connection
  (such as Demon or AOL)

Now...
- Launch your browser and connect up to the Internet
- Type in:
  http://www.digitaltimetraveller.co.uk/victorians
- Choose from the list of links to find out more about Victorians.

Museum sites

Beamish Open Air Museum
Beamish Open Air Museum homepage
The museum's website has a guide to its contents with special focus on the history of the railway.

National Maritime Museum
National Maritime Museum homepage
History of Great Britain as a seafaring nation, includes a trade and Empire quiz.

National Portrait Gallery
National Portrait Gallery Victorian collection
Their collection of subjects and people painted in Victorian times.

National Railway Museum
National Railway Museum homepage
Loads of information on the history of railways and trains – check out the Mallard, the fastest ever steam engine.

Ironbridge Museum
Ironbridge Museum homepage
A guide to the museum, events, and special kids section to explore.

National Waterways Museum
National Waterways Museum homepage
Find out about canals and barges across the UK, view their collections and find out about events.

Victoria and Albert Museum (V&A)
Victoria and Albert Museum homepage
An infodome, newsroom, learning zone and views of collections provide fantastic historical information and fun.

William Morris Gallery
William Morris Gallery homepage
A beautiful gallery of fabulous Victorian design, where you can download screen designs and more for your Victorian projects.

Sites for children

Time Strip
BBC
Overview of history with games, printouts and more.

The History of Cadburys
Cadbury Learning Zone
If you want to find out how this chocolate company started, then here is everything you need to know.

Canning Town
London Borough of Newham
The history of life in a Victorian industrial town.

Sainsbury's
Sainbury's Archive Virtual Museum
Another big company that was started up in Victorian times, and here is its history.

The Scrap Album
Malcolm Warrington
Loads of Victorian images for downloading and using in projects, as desktop designs, icons and more.

School's view of Victorian life
St Thomas' RC Primary School, Arbroath
St Thomas' School in Scotland have created their own site full of Victorian images and information.

Sites for teachers and parents

19th Century timeline
University of Minnesota, USA
Historical facts in chronological context.

English Heritage
English Heritage homepage
Pictures, links and information for sites across the country.

History Channel
The History Channel homepage
A fantastic resource site for history, with loads of information and ideas.

The London House
The London House homepage
The design and history of London's houses.

The Victorian Web
George P. Landow, Professor of English and Art History, Brown University
Resources and links to all things Victorian from religion and politics to science, technology, art and philosophy.

Victorian data

A Victorian lady's letters
Francis Barnard
Insights into Victorian life through the eyes of an intrepid Victorian lady who started as a children's governess and spent time in Burma as the wife of a District Commander.

Images of Queen Victoria
S Bishop
A growing collection of images of Queen Victoria and her extensive family.

Child labour
National Trust's Quarry Bank Mill
A view of workhouses, cheap labour and young apprentices in Victorian times.

Victorian census project
David Alan Gatley, Staffordshire University
Statistics on the people of Victorian Britain.

Victorian designs
Michele Grabowski
Use this site to inspire your own Victorian ideas, but if you want to download material you must make sure that you ask.

WARNING
The Internet is a public place and you need to be careful when exploring. Never go on-line without the permission of a parent or teacher.

Glossary

ABACUS   instrument with wooden balls on wires to calculate and do sums

ACTS OF PARLIAMENT laws passed by Parliament

BACTERIA   microscopic organisms, some of which can cause disease

BANQUET   dinner party or feast for lots of people

BLOOMERS   divided dresses invented in America, often used by lady cyclists

BOARD SCHOOL   primary schools set up by local boards of governors after the 1870 Education Act

BUTLER'S PANTRY   room where the butler of the house stored and cleaned the cutlery, glasses and silver

CLASS MONITOR young pupil who took on the role of teaching younger children

COOKING RANGE   large cast iron stove with hot plates and ovens often heated by a coal fires

COLLECTING DOG   real dog with a collecting tin (on a collar) for the widows and orphans of railway workers

CRIMEAN WAR   fought to stop Russia from taking new territories. The Russians were defeated in 1856

DATE PLAQUE   recorded the date and sometimes the name of the house on the front outside wall

DR BARNARDO   set up homes for orphaned children

EMPIRE   large group of countries in different parts of the world ruled by one country

FLUSHERS   were employed to clean the underground sewers

FOOD CHOPPER   kitchen utensil for mincing up food

GOLDEN JUBILEE was held to celebrate fifty years of Queen Victoria's reign

KID CATCHERS were employed to find children absent from school

MISSIONARY person who tries to convert others to their religion

OMNIBUS vehicle to carry numbers of passengers, now shortened to bus

PENNY BLACK the first postage stamp cost one penny

PENNY FARTHING bicycle named after the largest (penny) and the smallest (farthing) Victorian coins

QUACK pretends to offer proper medical advice and cures

RAILWAY MANIA period between 1844 and 1848 when large numbers of new railway lines were constructed

REFLECTING OVENS were placed in front of an open fire to cook meat, also called roasting screens or hasteners

REGINA Latin word for queen still used on coins today

SERVANTS' HALL room in large houses where all the servants took their meals together

STANDARDS classes in Victorian primary schools, from Standard 1 (aged 6) to Standard 6 (aged 11)

STANDARD TIME was Greenwich Mean Time (GMT) which replaced local time and was used by all railway companies in their timetables from 1852

SUNDAY BEST set of clothes kept aside for Sundays, especially for going to church

TOSHERS broke the law by searching for valuables lost in the underground sewers

TRAMS vehicles to carry passengers moving on rails through towns

Useful addresses

English Heritage
23 Savile Row
London W1S 2ET

TAG Learning Ltd
25 Pelham Road
Gravesend
Kent DA11 OHU

The four Victorian houses featured in Real Victorians are:

The Railway Village Museum
34 Faringdon Road
Swindon

Information from
Steam – Museum of the Great Western Railway
Kemble Drive
Swindon SN2 2TA

Brodsworth Hall (English Heritage)
Brodsworth, 5m NW of Doncaster off A635
South Yorkshire DN5 7XJ

Down House (English Heritage)
Luxted Road
Downe
Kent BR6 7JT

Osborne House (English Heritage)
SE of East Cowes
Isle of Wight PO32 6JY

Other places to visit
You will also find information if you connect to the special website for this book (see page 44). Here is a list of some of the houses and museums which have Victorian collections:

Buckingham Palace, London, is open during the summer.

Castle Museum, York has a reconstruction of a Victorian street.

Fox Talbot Museum, Lacock, Wiltshire has collections related to the Victorian photographer W H Fox Talbot.

Hitchin British Schools in Hertfordshire has reconstructed Victorian school rooms.

Ironbridge Gorge, Shropshire, has a number of museums and reconstructed Victorian houses and other buildings (including a public house, a printers workshop and an undertakers).

Museum of Childhood, Edinburgh, has many Victorian objects including toys and games. Museum of London has reconstructed Victorian shops as well as objects to see.

Museum of Science and Industry, Manchester, has a reconstruction of a Victorian sewer which can be visited.

Museum of Welsh Life, Cardiff has reconstruction Victorian houses and a school.

National Maritime Museum, Greenwich, The Science Museum, Kensington and the Victoria and Albert Museum, Kensington all have Victorian collections to visit in London.

National Railway Museum, York has large collections including a carriage from Victoria's royal train.

The North of England Open Air Museum at Beamish in County Durham has reconstructed Victorian buildings including a school.

Port Sunlight, Merseyside has houses built for factory workers open to visit.

Ragged School Museum, Bow, London has a reconstructed classroom.

Steam – Museum of the Great Western Railway, Swindon has large collections and from there you can visit the railway worker's house featured in this book.

Ulster Folk and Transport Museum has large collections and reconstructed buildings.

Weald and Downland Open Air Museum, near Chichester has reconstructed buildings of all periods which include a Victorian school.

Wigan Pier Heritage Centre, Wigan, Lancashire has a working Victorian schoolroom.

Windsor Castle, Berkshire is also the place where Victoria and Albert are buried (mausoleum in the park).

**Answers to the mystery objects on page 43:
1 for buffing finger nails to make them shiny. 2 tin opener. 3 jelly mould. 4 tin can for carrying hot water. 5 ink pot. 6 cigar lighter. 7 torch. 8 jar for pouring ink. 9 knife cleaner. 10 for pressing food through a sieve. 11 refrigerator. 12 for mending gloves.**